Shots & Shooter Drink Recipes

THE BARTENDER'S GUIDE TO TASTY "LITTLE" COCKTAILS

How to be a Star
Behind the Shooter Bar

Written By:
Bazooka Joe

Legal Drinking Age Required:

You must be of legal drinking age to access this book. Straight Shooters Marketing does not promote underage drinking. By accessing this book, you swear and affirm that you are over the age of 21. Straight Shooters Marketing makes every effort to ensure that alcoholic beverages are not delivered to, nor served to, anyone who is under the age of 21. If you do not agree with these conditions of use please do not access this book.

Government Warning Concerning Health Consequences of Consuming Alcohol:
By accessing this book, you acknowledge that there is a government warning concerning the health effects of consuming alcoholic beverages.
Government warning: *(1) According to the Surgeon General, women should not drink alcoholic beverages during pregnancy because of the risk of birth defects. (2) Consumption of alcoholic beverages impairs your ability to drive a car or operate machinery and may cause health problems.*

Drink responsibly. Never drink and drive.

Liability Waiver:
In consideration for your being given access to material herein, you hereby release, waive, discharge and covenant not to sue Bazooka Joe, the Company, Straight Shooters Marketing, its subsidiaries, DBAs, affiliates, successors, contractors, agents, representatives and/or employees from any and all liability, claims, demands, actions and causes of action whatsoever arising out of or relating to any damage to your property or loss, damage or injury that you personally sustain, including death, whether caused by the negligence of the Company or its representatives or not while participating in Company programs, using Site content or material and/or attending Company Events in person or online, regardless of location. You hereby assume all risks to your property and your person and in no way will Bazooka Joe, the shooter books, the site Shooter Roulette or the Company, Straight Shooters Marketing be liable to you for damages or injuries you might sustain.

If you do not agree with these conditions of use please do not access this book.

ISBN 9798510098815

SHOTS & SHOOTER DRINK RECIPIES - *THE BARTENDER'S GUIDE TO TASTY "LITTLE" COCKTAILS*
IS PROTECTED BY COPYRIGHT © 1987
STRAIGHT SHOOTERS MARKETING
ALL RIGHTS RESERVED

WWW.SHOOTERROULETTE.COM
FOR MORE INFORMATION, EMAIL:
INFO@SHOOTERROULETTE.COM

NO PART OF THIS BOOK MAY BE REPRODUCED IN ANY FORM WHATSOEVER WITHOUT WRITTEN PERMISSION FROM STRAIGHT SHOOTERS MARKETING

PURCHASE OF THIS BOOK PROVIDES PERMANENT ACCESS TO THE ONLINE SHOOTER DIRECTORY AT WWW.SHOOTERROULETTE.COM
NOW YOU CAN TAKE THE PARTY WITH YOU.

COVER DESIGN AND LAYOUT BY
RILEY MILLER
INFO@SKYMILLZ.COM

For Mary.

*"Momma always told me not to look into
The sights of the sun. But Momma,
That's where the fun is."*

— Bruce Springsteen
Blinded By The Light

Shots & Shooters

TABLE OF CONTENTS

Introduction To Shooters	1
Liqueur Production Methods	3
Basic Liqueur Types	5-16
Tips And Tricks	17
Alphabetical Guide To 101 Shooters	19-22
101 Shooters	23-73
Ounces of Prevention	74
Hangover Helpers	75
Stocking Your Shooter Bar	80

*"Alcohol might be man's worst enemy,
But the Bible says, love your enemy."*
- Frank Sinatra

*"Let schoolmasters puzzle their brain,
With grammar, and nonsense, and learning,
Good liquor, I stoutly maintain,
Gives genius a better discerning."*
— Oliver Goldsmith

Shots & Shooters

INTRODUCTION TO SHOOTERS

For centuries, people from all corners of the world have been concocting and drinking liqueurs. Many countries lay claim to being the first to make liqueurs but all agree that it wasn't until the Middle Ages that their use became prominent. Sorcerers, wizards, alchemists and monks became proficient at making consistent products that boasted life prolonging benefits. The Black Death had swept through Europe so it was no surprise that demand quickly grew for these 'elixirs of eternal life'.

In addition to these medicinal properties, liqueurs gained renown as aphrodisiacs. Kings and commoners alike used these highly potent, secret potions to reduce inhibitions and increase passions.

"It (drink) provokes the desire
But it takes away the performance."
- Shakespeare (Macbeth)

In more recent years, liqueurs joined in a concert of colour and taste have become known as shooters. They still cool inhibitions and inflame passions. Indeed, their popularity at any social function has made them the "Champagne Of A New Generation". Today many, who previously may have shunned a straight shot, are now raising a shooter in a toast of good cheer.

Shots & Shooters

Custom dictates that shooters be consumed in the following manner. First, a brief toast or witty quote is proposed (many are presented later in this book), usually by the person who bought or ordered the round. Next the shooter glasses are raised and 'clinked' together in unison. The bell-like sound was once thought to ward off the devil.

Finally the best part; the shooter is downed in one fell swoop.

*"Drink to the men who connect you to life.
Drink, drink, raise your glass,
Raise your glass higher."*

— David Bowie
(Station to Station)

In writing this guide, I have attempted to provide recipes worth dipping into for entertainment and education. It is intended for both the professional and amateur bartender and hopefully all will find it factual and comprehensive. That being said, I now cancel all bets, break all guarantees, ensure no conclusions and disclaim any and all liability incurred by the use and/or abuse of the information presented herein. You are your own liquor control board.

Shots & Shooters

LIQUEUR PRODUCTION METHODS

This section will explain some complex production methods in simple layman's terms. Some technical experts may take offense to my simplifications, but my aim is to foster interest, not create more technical experts.

Simply stated, a liqueur is a flavourful distilled spirit containing a minimum of 2.5% sugar by weight. This works out to about 1 ½ tablespoons of sugar in a standard 750ml bottle.

Most liqueurs are made in the same basic way. Spirits are mixed with sugar or a sugar syrup and natural flavourings. These flavourings can take the form of fruits, herbs, seeds, flowers and spices. Even bark is used in some instances. Most distillers employ a secret combination of these natural flavourings to create their signature brands.

There are three main methods to produce or generate these flavourings:

- **PERCOLATION**
- **INFUSION**
- **DISTILLATION**

PERCOLATION is a method similar to the way in which you brew your morning coffee. Spirits are put in a large tank and the flavouring sources are placed in a large basket-like container at the top of the tank. The spirits are then pumped up to the top where they are sprayed over the mixture and dripped back down to the bottom. The process is repeated over and over until all the flavour, colour and aroma has been extracted from the leaves, seeds and herbs.

Shots & Shooters

The INFUSION method is used primarily for making fruit flavours. The fruit is placed directly into the spirits and left for a period of time to soak and steep until the flavour, aroma and colour has been extracted. Maceration is a similar method but with this type of infusion the ingredients are mashed before they are left to soak and steep.

For most liqueurs, infusion or percolation is only the first step. Once the flavour has been extracted, the mixture is then distilled to give it more delicate, smoother taste.

"Fair thought and happy hours attend on you."
  - Shakespeare (Merchant Of Venice)

In some instances the DISTILLATION method is used alone. The flavouring source and the spirits are placed in a still and heated. As the mixture is heated, the alcohol turns to a vapour and rises, leaving the water behind. The entire process works because alcohol boils at a lower temperature (172°F) than water (212°F). As the alcoholic vapours cool, they condense back into a liquid form. This liquid or distillate retains the flavour of the various flavouring ingredients.

The base for most liqueurs is a neutral alcohol, which is tasteless and odorless. With these types, the flavour of the final product comes only from the flavouring sources. However, some liqueurs use brandy, whiskey, scotch, rum or bourbon as their base. These, of course, contribute significantly to the final taste.

Shots & Shooters

BASIC LIQUEUR TYPES
(SPECIFIC GRAVITY CAN VARY BY BRAND, SEE PAGE 18)

CHOCOLATE
Chocolate Suisse *(107)*
Godiva Dark Chocolate *(106)*
Swiss Chocolate Almond *(106)*

CREAM
Amarula *(105)*
Bailey's *(106)*
Haagen Dazs *(107)*
Myer's Rum Cream *(105)*

FRUIT
Apricot *(109)*
Banana *(112)*
Coconut *(104)*
Melon *(105)*

NUT
Amaretto *(108)*
Frangelico *(106)*

COFFEE
Copa De Oro *(111)*
Kahlua *(116)*
Tia Maria *(109)*

CREME DE MENTHE
Peppermint Schnapps
(103-112 Varies)

LICORICE
Ouzo *(109)*
Pernod *(110)*
Sambuca *(109)*

ORANGE
Cointreau *(104)*
Grand Curacao *(108)*
Grand Marnier *(103)*

★ OLD FAMILY SECRETS ★

Benedictine *(107)*
Chambord *(113)*
Chartreuse *(99)*
Drambuie *(108)*
Galliano *(110)*

Glayva *(109)*
Irish Mist *(104)*
Parfait A'mour *(113)*
Southern Comfort *(97)*
Yukon Jack *(100)*

CHOCOLATE LIQUEURS

These liqueurs are percolated from cocoa and vanilla beans using a base of neutral spirits. The most popular in this class are the light (clear) and dark (brown) creme de cocao's. In recent years many distillers have started making liqueurs that combine chocolate with such traditional flavours as cherry, coconut and mint.

BRANDS

CHOCOLATE SUISSE
A chocolate flavoured Swiss liqueur produced with miniature squares of chocolate afloat in the bottle.

GODIVA DARK CHOCOLATE LIQUEUR
Since 1926 these famous Belgian chocolatiers have made this liqueur with black cherries, orange peels, coffee and unsweetened dark chocolate.

SWISS CHOCOLATE ALMOND
A rich, smooth liqueur that combines many cocaos, almonds and vanilla.

Shots & Shooters

COFFEE LIQUEURS

Percolation is the usual method of producing this very popular class of liqueurs. The coffee beans create a distinct rich taste and a strong aromatic fragrance.

BRANDS

COPA DE ORO

This imported coffee liqueur is made with Mexican beans and some of the world's most delicate and rare spices. A new player but it is the fastest growing product in this category.

KAHLUA

For years this has been the number one imported liqueur. It's made from mexican coffee beans, neutral spirits and sugar syrup.

TIA MARIA

This is made from a two hundred year old recipe of Jamaican coffee extracts and a neutral spirit base. It is lighter in density than Kahlua and is therefore best suited for shaken rather than layered shooters.

Shots & Shooters

CREAM LIQUEURS

Traditionally, these liqueurs were made with Irish whiskey, fresh dairy cream from the southern coast of Ireland, chocolate and just a touch of coffee. Some relative newcomers have altered this recipe by utilizing different spirit bases. The results have been nothing short of spectacular.

Shake well before using and refrigerate after opening.

BRANDS

AMARULA
South African entry, made with the ripened fruit of the Marula tree.

BAILEY'S
The traditional Irish cream liqueur.

HAAGEN DAZS
A tasty blend of Dutch cream and a cognac base.

MYER'S RUM CREAM
Here, it's a smooth caramel taste derived from a base of Jamaican rum that makes it a personal favorite for shooters, cocktails and coffee drinks.

Shots & Shooters

CREME DE MENTHE LIQUEURS

This refreshing liqueur holds the cool flavour of natural mint and is available in white (clear) and green.

Over the last decade, minty creme de menthe liqueurs have given way to lighter "schnapps", in particular flavoured ones like apple and peach. Peach schnapps created quite a stir in the liquor industry back in 1985, when over one million cases were shipped - the greatest number ever for a new product.

Other flavours available besides peach, include root beer, licorice, pear, raspberry, passion fruit and even kiwi. Incidentally, "schnapps" in german refers to any water-white distilled beverage alcohol.

PEPPERMINT SCHNAPPS
Both dry and water-white, it has a very pleasant peppermint flavour. Schnapps is lighter-bodied and not as sweet as Creme de Menthe but it is ideal for most recipes.

FAVOURITE FLAVOURS
Peach
Butterscotch
Pear
Chocolate

Shots & Shooters

FRUIT LIQUEURS

The flavouring is created by infusion or maceration of fruit or fruit spirits. The base can take the form of brandy, rum or whiskey but in most cases a neutral alcohol is used.

POPULAR TYPES

All the major distillers offer a wide selection of fruit liqueurs. The quality can vary greatly but most are fun to experiment with. Some of the more interesting are:

APRICOT
Well balanced and versatile, Apricot has a slight vanilla overtone.

BANANA
A sweet, yellow liqueur with the full flavour of ripe bananas. A must for any shooter bar.

COCONUT
Delicious and tropical, coconut is often made with a rum base.

MELON
Usually bright green in colour, this liqueur has the interesting taste of melon and honeydews.

Shots & Shooters

LICORICE LIQUEURS

These sweet, delicately aromatic liqueurs all have a pleasant licorice flavour. The major type, Anisette, derives its licorice quality from anise seeds but additional flavourings can be used (for example citrus peels) to complete the final taste. Anisette is produced all over the world and the taste will vary greatly with the extra flavourings used by each distiller.

ASSOCIATED TYPES

SAMBUCA

An Italian creation similar in taste to Anisette but tempered with the seeds of the witch elderberry bush in a brandy base. For those in the know - there is really only one brand to use; Luxardo.

PERNOD

The liqueur is derived from the distillation rather than the maceration of the anise seeds. A fine french brandy base forms a smooth overall taste.

OUZO

A potent Greek creation that's dry and fairly harsh, with a high alcohol content. BEWARE - Don't smoke and keep away from open flame.

NUT LIQUEURS

Nut liqueurs use a variety of fruit pits, kernels and nuts as their primary flavouring source. Other items serve as secondary sources such as fruit pulp, citrus, peels, chocolate, coffee, vanilla and herbs. They are usually infused or macerated.

POPULAR TYPES

AMARETTO
A smooth, naturally sweet almond taste created from peach and apricot pits and, of course, almonds. Originally from Saronno, Italy, several are now made in North America.

FRANGELICO
Another Italian creation that uses hazelnuts with flowers and berries as the flavouring sources.

PISTACCHIO
An Italian cream liqueur made with pistacchios.

Shots & Shooters

ORANGE LIQUEURS

The orange flavouring is usually made from a mixture of various orange peels infused in neutral spirits. Orange liqueurs or Triple Sec's differ in their degree of tanginess (citrus content), alcohol content, dryness and spirit base.

BRANDS

COINTREAU
A brand name, Triple Sec is made from a blend of bitter and sweet orange peels from the West Indies. It is French in origin and white (clear) in colour.

GRAND MARNIER
A bottle of G.M. is sold every second of every day and the reason for these healthy sales is quality. Every bottle is washed with a form of unsweetened G.M. to prevent any dilution and each label is quality checked for position by laser. With this kind of intense commitment to excellence it's easy to see why only the finest cognac and the best bitter, green, orange peels from Haiti are used.

GRAND CURACAO
Similar to Grand Marnier, Curacao has more sugar, sweet oranges and spices. It's named after the West Indian island where the oranges originate.

Shots & Shooters

OLD FAMILY RECIPES

These brands have been popular for ages in their homelands and today enjoy international recognition and acceptance.

BRANDS

ADVOKAAT
A rich, sweet Dutch eggnog of low alcohol content, flavoured with coffee and a variety of spices including vanilla.

BENEDICTINE
French monks have been making this liqueur since the 1500's. This secret formula of bark, roots and over 200 herbs is only known to three people at any one time. It's ingredients are macerated in brandy, distilled twice and aged in oak casks.

CHARTREUSE
Another well kept secret recipe that contains the flavourings of over 130 herbs, flowers and fruits. During the French Revolution, many Carthusian monks took their precious secret to the grave rather than reveal it to their captors.

DRAMBUIE
The name translates to "the drink that satisfies". This legendary Scottish recipe of scotch, heather, honey and herbs was given to the MacKinnon family by Bonnie Prince Charlie for saving his life after the fall of the Stuarts (1745).

Shots & Shooters

GLAYVA
A sweet, smooth mixture of scotch, honey and herbs, similar to Drambuie and also from Scotland.

IRISH MIST
This mixture of Irish Whiskey, honey, herbs and clover has been known for over 1000 years as "Heather Wine".

PARFAIT A'MOUR
A sweet concoction of violets, rose petals, vanilla and citrus peels make Parfait A'mour a must for any shooter bar. The name translates to "perfect love" and it was once the preferred drink of Parisian prostitutes.

LIQUORE GALLIANO
A secret Italian recipe of 80 spices, herbs and fruits that produces a taste similar to a mild yet thick anisette.

SOUTHERN COMFORT
A U.S. creation of peaches, oranges and herbs with a neutral base. Made famous in the 1960's as Janis Joplin's favourite liqueur.

YUKON JACK
"The Black Sheep of Canadian liquors" is made with a blend of Canadian rye whiskeys, herbs and subtle citrus flavours.

MISCELLANEOUS SPIRITS

CHAMBORD

Chambord is a french liqueur made of red and black raspberries, vanilla from madagascar, citrus, honey, and cognac.

COGNAC

The premier brandy of France that comes from a limited area surrounding the ancient city of Cognac. Only brandy distilled from grapes grown within this area may be called cognac.

BOURBON

This corn whiskey has been called "The Great Spirit Of America". There are strict requirements for a whiskey to be called a bourbon. For instance, the grain mixture must contain 51% corn and the final product must be aged a minimum of two years in charred oak casks.

TEQUILA

Although a relative new export for Mexico (1947), it has been around Mexico City since the days of the Aztecs. Tequila is distilled from the mezcal plant and it bears no relationship to the hallucinogen mescaline nor to the plant Mescal. This fable still continues today but tequila is no more a drug than other liqueurs or liquors.
Tequila comes in white (clear) and gold, which gets its colour from aging in oak casks.

Shots & Shooters

TIPS & TRICKS I'VE LEARNED IN FRONT OF AND BEHIND BARS

★ To pour and layer shooters, fit your bottles with standard bar speed spouts. Control the flow of the liqueur by manipulating your forefinger over the spout. With your other hand, hold a maraschino cherry or a teaspoon and slowly pour over the cherry or the back of a teaspoon.

★ When layering shooters always pour lighter liqueurs over heavier, thicker ones.

★ Never drink anything that is lit and on fire. Drinks of this nature date back to the middle ages and are called "Flap Dragons". They didn't know any better back then, but we do now, so leave the fire-eating act to the circus people.

★ Current trends indicate a preference for shooters to be shaken rather than poured. Therefore, you may wish to pick up a bartender's drink shaker and ice strainer.

★ Never force a shooter on anyone.
"One man's drink is another man's poison."

★ **NEVER DRINK AND DRIVE**
It's far cheaper to hire a cab than a lawyer.

Shots & Shooters

SPECIFIC GRAVITY

Everything you need to know with respect to specific gravity is contained in one sentence:

*The higer the specific gravity,
the thicker the liqueur,
the closer to the bottom.*

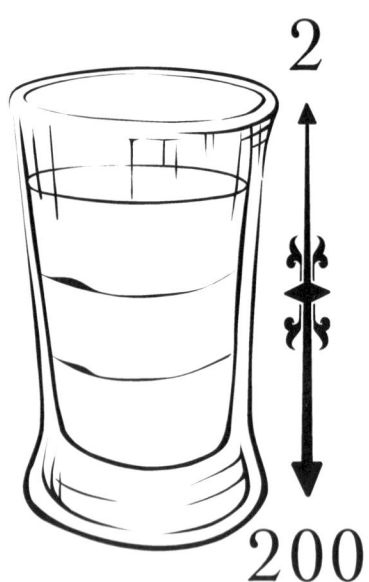

*"I have made it a rule -
Never to drink by daylight, and never to
refuse a drink after dark."*

— H.L. Mencken

Shots & Shooters

ONE HUNDRED & ONE SHOOTERS

A.B.C.	Blue Hawaii
After Eight	Blue Jay
Alter Ego	Brave Bull
Amaretto Sour	B 52
Apple Carts	B 53
Apple Jacks	Chanel 69
Arctic Front	Cherry Bomb
Banana Sandwich	Cherry Root Beer
Banana Split	China White
Bazooka Joe	Chocolate Chip
Beached Whale	Chocolate Monk
Belize Breeze	Cocoknot
Black Jelly Bean	Coma
Black Forest Cake	Creamsicle
Blowjob	Double Jack

Shots & Shooters

ONE HUNDRED & ONE SHOOTERS

Electric Banana	Landslide
Electric Popsicle	Laserbeam
Fifty Second Avenue	Leprechaun's Lunch
French Connection	Letter Bomb
Fruit Basket	Licorice Lix
Fudgesicle	Licorice Twist
Furburissor	Little Alex
Gatoraider	Little Russian
Green Machine	Lorraytoes
Good Night Kiss	Melonball
Guam Bomb	Methanol
Heroin	Mexican Chiller
Icicle	Mexican Snowshoe
Kamikaze	Nishka Lishka
Kicker	Nutcracker

Shots & Shooters

ONE HUNDRED & ONE SHOOTERS

Oreo Cookie	Sicilian Kiss
Orgasm	Slippery Nipple
P.C.B.	Snakebite
Peppermint Pushover	Speakeasy
Popsicle	Spiked Heel
Prairie Fire	Strawberry Fields
Red Jelly Bean	Tartan Special
Rusty Spike	Test-Tube Baby
Ryan's Rush	Tequila Slammer
Sambuca	Turbo
Sambuca Depth Charge	Tutti Fruitti Punch
Schnapps	Watergate
Screaming Lizard	Windmill
Seven Forty Seven	X-Ray
Sex On The Beach	Zipper

ONE HUNDRED & ONE SHOOTERS

HOT SHOTS

After Eight	Meltdown
Apollo	Mocha Magic
Campfire	Mini Marnier
Canada Cup	Ski Lift
Jack Frost	Yeti's Revenge
Kilt Warmer	

RATINGS

SKIP
Mentioned here more as a courtesy than a recommendation.

MACHO
Try when you're feeling brave.

PRETTY
More interesting than tasty.

TASTY
And probably addictive.

OUTSTANDING
Not to be missed.

Shots & Shooters

A.B.C.
★★★

Pour:

⅓ Nut Liqueur
⅓ Cream Liqueur
⅓ Orange Liqueur

Traditionally made with Amaretto, Bailey's and Cointreau.

"I drink to the general joy Of the whole table."
- Shakespeare

AFTER EIGHT
★★★★

Pour:

½ Coffee Liqueur
⅓ Green Creme de Menthe
⅙ Cream

Like the mint, this is the perfect finish to that special dinner.

Shots & Shooters

ALTER EGO
★★★★

Pour:

⅓ Chocolate Liqueur
⅓ Cream Liqueur
⅓ Orange Liqueur

A subtle variation of the B-52.

*"No animal ever created anything
So bad as drunkeness,
Or so good as drink."*

— G.K. Chesterton

AMARETTO SOUR
★★★

Shake:

½ Nut Liqueur (Amaretto)
⅓ Lime Juice
⅙ Cream

An interesting change from the ordinary.

For those who enjoy Whiskey Sours, Tom Collins', or Daiquiris.

Shots & Shooters

APPLE CARTS
★★★★
Shake:

½ Apple Schnapps
⅔ Peach Schnapps

Knock it over and you've had enough.

*"They speak of my drinking
But never think of my thirst."*
- Scottish Proverb

APPLE JACKS
★★
Pour:

½ Jack Daniels
½ Apple Schnapps

Not for breakfast.

Shots & Shooters

ARCTIC FRONT
★★

Shake Vigorously:

½ Yukon Jack
½ Vodka

Guaranteed to keep the cold out, and the heat in on long Canadian winters.

"Every man on earth comes to the time when He's more interested in liquor than in women. But Canadian men seem to come to it rather early."
— **Richard J. Needham**

BANANA SANDWICH
★★★★★

Pour:

½ Coffee Liqueur
⅓ Banana Liqueur
⅙ Cream Liqueur

Also called a monkey's lunch. Either way, it's a very tasty shooter.

Shots & Shooters

BANANA SPLIT
★★★★

Shake:

⅔ Banana Liqueur
⅓ Cream Liqueur

Even better than the ones you had as a child, and it also makes a great dessert topping.

"Too much of a good thing can be wonderful."
- Mae West

BAZOOKA JOE
★★★★★

Shake:

½ Parfait A'mour
(Sub Chambord or Bols Blue)
⅓ Banana Liqueur
⅙ Cream Liqueur

It's the bubble-gum taste that makes this shooter so popular.

*Parfait A'mour can be hard to find

BEACHED WHALE
★★★

Pour:

½ Clear Chocolate Liqueur
(eg. White Cocao)
½ Clear Orange Liqueur
(eg. Triple Sec)
Slowly add ½ capful of Advokaat.

A difficult shooter to make but an excellent presentation when done correctly.

"I always keep a supply of stimulant handy in case I see a snake - which I also keep handy."
                                                              - W.C. Fields

BELIZE BREEZE
★★★★

Shake:

½ Tequila
½ Nut Liqueur
Splash Pineapple Juice

A sure-fire cure for a heatwave.

Shots & Shooters

BLACK JELLY BEAN
★★★★

Pour:

⅙ Grenadine
½ Licorice Liqueur
(a heavy or dense one)
⅓ Parfait A'mour
*(Sub Chambord or Bols Blue)

A pretty red, clear violet presentation.

*Parfait A'mour can be hard to find

> "Any club that would accept me as a member, I wouldn't want to join."
> - Julies (Groucho) Marx

BLACK FOREST CAKE
★★★★

Shake:

⅓ Chocolate Liqueur
⅓ Cherry Liqueur
⅙ Cream Liqueur
⅙ Sherry

A special, new dessert option.

Shots & Shooters

BLOWJOB
★★★★

Shake:

½ Coffee Liqueur
⅓ Licorice Liqueur
⅙ Cream Liqueur
Top with a dash of whipped cream.

The fun part is drinking this one - with no hands!

> *"A club is a place where a gentleman Can get drunk respectably."*
> **- Peter McArthur**

BLUE HAWAII
★★★

Shake:

⅓ Parfait A'mour
⅓ Coconut Liqueur
⅓ Cream

A "luau" favourite.

Shots & Shooters

BLUE JAY
★★★

Shake:

⅓ Parfait A'mour
⅓ Banana Liqueur
⅓ Peppermint Schnapps

OK, OK! Blue Jays, Blue Jays! Let's have shots!

"What a man considers indecent is an important Clue to his character."

- Robertson Davis

BRAVE BULL
★★

Shake:

⅓ Coffee Liqueur
⅔ Tequila

This is what makes grown Mexican men go into a ring and challenge a two-thousand pound bull.

Shots & Shooters

B 52
★★★★

Pour:

⅓ Coffee Liqueur
⅓ Cream Liqueur
⅓ Orange Liqueur

The original shooter.

"Drinking must be practiced with great prudence. A man who exposes himself when he is intoxicated, Has not the art of getting drunk."

- Samuel Johnson

B 53
★

Pour:

½ Coffee Liqueur
⅓ Licorice Liqueur
⅙ Orange Liqueur

A variation of this recipe calls for tequila rather than licorice liqueur. Either way, this is one to avoid.

Shots & Shooters

CHANEL 69
★★★

Shake:

⅓ Banana Liqueur
⅓ Cream Liqueur
⅓ Advokaat

Like the perfume, very popular at Christmas.

> *"Wearing underwear is as formal as I ever hope to get."*
> - W. Knox Haynes

CHERRY BOMB
★★

Pour:

⅓ Coffee Liqueur
⅓ Cream Liqueur
⅙ Banana Liqueur
⅙ Cherry Liqueur

A real firecracker.

Shots & Shooters

CHERRY ROOT BEER
★★★★

Shake:

⅔ Root Beer Schnapps
⅓ Cherry Liqueur

For an even wilder taste add some chocolate liqueur for a chocolate, cherry root beer.

"I drink to make other people interesting."
- George Jean Nathan

CHINA WHITE
★★★★

Shake:

½ White Cocao
½ Cream Liqueur

Topped with a sprinkle of cinnamon.

Shots & Shooters

CHOCOLATE CHIP
★★★★★

Pour:

½ Chocolate Liqueur
⅓ Peppermint Schnapps
⅙ Cream Liqueur
Option: Top with whipped cream

Just like the cookies, these disappear fast.

*"So eat, drink and be merry
Have a good time if you will.
But God help you when the time comes,
Any of you have to foot the bill."*
— Robert Service 1907

CHOCOLATE MONK
★★★★★

Shake:

½ Chocolate Liqueur
⅓ Nut Liqueur
⅙ Cream Liqueur

Traditionally made with Frangelico, hence the name.

Shots & Shooters

COCOKNOT
★★★

Shake:

⅓ Coffee Liqueur
⅓ Coconut Liqueur
⅓ Cointreau

Makes a great tropical cooler when mixed and shaken with cream.

"There is hope for the man who can occasionally Make a spontaneous and irrevocable ass of himself."
— Peter McArthur

COMA
★★★

Shake:

⅓ Coffee Liqueur
⅓ Orange Liqueur
⅓ Banana Liqueur

Too many and you're out.

Shots & Shooters

CREAMSICLE
★★★★

Shake:

⅓ Orange Liqueur
⅙ Nut Liqueur
⅙ Cream Liqueur
⅓ Orange Juice

Also makes an excellent milkshake/cocktail by blending with some cream and ice.

"I've made an ass of myself so many times I often wonder if I am one."

— Norman Mailer

DOUBLE JACK
★★

Shake:

½ Jack Daniels
½ Yukon Jack

A must for bourbon drinkers.

Shots & Shooters

ELECTRIC BANANA
★★

Shake:

⅓ Tequila
⅔ Banana Liqueur

Shocking.

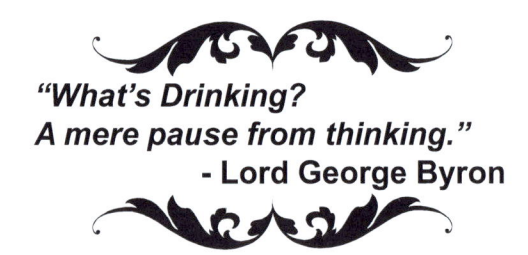

*"What's Drinking?
A mere pause from thinking."*
- Lord George Byron

ELECTRIC POPSICLE
★★★★

Shake:

⅓ Parfait A'mour
(Sub Chambord or Bols Blue)
⅓ Banana Liqueur
⅙ Vodka
⅙ Lime Juice

Also known as a Blue Popsicle.

*Parfait A'mour can be hard to find

Shots & Shooters

FIFTY SECOND AVENUE
★★★

Shake:

⅓ Pear Liqueur
⅓ Cream Liqueur
⅓ Banana Liqueur

Classy, colourful and tasty.

"I drink no more than a sponge."
- Francois Rabelais

FRENCH CONNECTION
★

Shake:

½ Brandy
½ Orange Liqueur

This is what really hurt Popeye Doyle in Marseille.

Shots & Shooters

FRUIT BASKET
★★★★

Shake:

¼ Banana Liqueur
¼ Apricot Liqueur
¼ Cream Liqueur
¼ Pear Liqueur

Suitable for your sick friends in hospital although delivery can prove difficult.

"A little too much is just right."
- Grips Comic Almanac 1883

FUDGESICLE
★★★★

Pour:

⅓ Chocolate Liqueur
⅓ Cream Liqueur
⅙ Banana Liqueur
⅙ Cream

Better than the original.

Shots & Shooters

FURBURISSOR

★★★★

Shake:

⅓ Licorice Liqueur
⅓ Banana Liqueur
⅓ Cream

White in colour but never innocent.

*"A very, merry, dancing, drinking,
Laughing, quaffing, and unthinking time."*
— John Dryden

GATORAIDER

★★★

Shake:

⅓ Banana Liqueur
⅓ Strawberry Liqueur
⅓ Cherry Liqueur

For a quick boost.

Shots & Shooters

GREEN MACHINE
★★★

Shake:

⅓ Green Creme de Menthe
⅓ Banana Liqueur
⅓ Cream Liqueur

For those with a very sweet tooth.

*"The rapturous, wild and ineffable pleasure
Of drinking at somebody else's expense."*
- H.S Leigh

GOOD NIGHT KISS
★★★★

Shake:

⅓ Coffee Liqueur
⅓ Cream Liqueur
⅓ Cream

This shooter is always the start of something sexy.

Shots & Shooters

GUAM BOMB
★★★

Shake:

⅓ Coffee Liqueur
⅓ Cream Liqueur
⅓ Coconut Liqueur

⅓ of this tiny island is devoted to U.S. military installations.

"Money is a good thing to have In these twisted times."
— Hunter S. Thompson

HEROIN
★

Shake:

½ Orange Liqueur
½ Licorice Liqueur

It's not as bad as it sounds - it's worse.

Shots & Shooters

ICICLE
★★★

Shake:

⅓ Peppermint Schnapps
⅓ Vodka
⅓ Cointreau

Serve very, very cold.

"I've been rich and I've been poor and Believe me, rich is better."
- Joe E. Lewis

KAMIKAZE
★★★

Shake:

⅔ Vodka or Tequila
⅓ Lime Juice

Rarely ordered by a sober person.

Shots & Shooters

KICKER
★★★

Shake:

⅓ Coffee Liqueur
⅓ Nut Liqueur
⅓ Orange Liqueur

A game winner.

*"I was never drunk enough,
Never poor enough,
Never rich enough."*
— Leonard Cohen

LANDSLIDE
★★★★

Pour:

⅓ Banana Liqueur
⅓ Cream Liqueur
⅓ Orange Liqueur

Feel the earth move under your feet
(And kiss the beach house goodbye).

LASERBEAM
★

Shake:

½ Tequila
½ Galliano

Phasers on stun.

"Who needs money when you're funny."
— Randy Newman

LEPRECHAUN'S LUNCH
★★★★

Pour:

½ Coffee Liqueur
⅓ Green Creme de Menthe
⅙ Cream Liqueur

Must be shaken on March 17th - Saint Patrick's Day.

Shots & Shooters

LETTERBOMB
★

Shake:

⅓ Irish Whiskey
⅓ Irish Mist
⅓ Irish Cream Liqueur

Sudden, unexpected and dangerous.

"I always have trouble remembering Three things: faces, names and I can't Remember what the third thing is."
— Fred Allen

LICORICE LIX
★★★

Shake:

¾ Licorice Liqueur
¼ Orange Juice

Also makes an interesting cocktail by adding a good shot of orange juice and ice.

LICORICE TWIST
★★★★

Shake:

½ Coffee Liqueur
⅓ Licorice Liqueur
⅙ Cream Liqueur

Candy for grown-ups.

"Remember the poor - it costs nothing."
- Josh Billings

LITTLE ALEX
★★★

Shake:

½ Coffee Liqueur
⅓ Brandy
⅙ Cream

Real nasty horror show, O my brothers.

Shots & Shooters

LITTLE RUSSIAN
★★

Shake:

½ Coffee Liqueur
½ Vodka

Sometimes called a "Little Black Russian".

*"Blessed are the young,
For they shall inherit the national debt."*
— Herbert Hoover

LORRAYTOES
★★★

Shake:

⅓ Nut Liqueur
⅓ Southern Comfort
⅓ Cream Liqueur

Named after the 'Wild Woman' of the O.K. Valley.

Shots & Shooters

MELONBALL
★★★

Shake:

⅔ Melon Liqueur
⅓ Pineapple Juice

Vodka is an optional ingredient. Also makes a great cocktail.

"The hardest thing in the world to Understand is the income tax."
- Albert Einstein

METHANOL
★

Shake:

½ Mentholated Schnapps
½ Drambuie

A kind of 'supercharged' turbo

Shots & Shooters

MEXICAN CHILLER
★★

Shake:

¾ Tequila
¼ Clamato Juice
Several drops of Tabasco

A mild form of the Prairie Fire.
Often used as a hangover 'cure'.

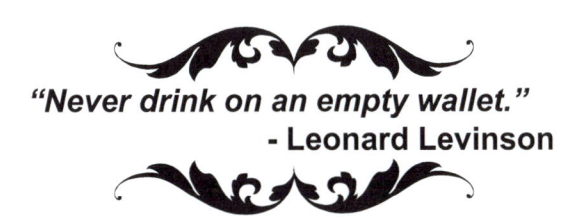

"Never drink on an empty wallet."
- Leonard Levinson

MEXICAN SNOWSHOE
★★★

Pour:

½ Peppermint Schnapps
½ Tequila

Makes a great optical illusion of falling snow when made correctly.

Shots & Shooters

NISHKA-LISHKA
★★★

Pour:

1 Cognac
1 orange or lemon "citrus wheel"

Coat one side with instant coffee and the other side with sugar.

Fold in half.
Drink, then bite into the folded citrus wheel.

A favorite with bartenders after a busy night.

"May you be merry and lack nothing."
- Shakespeare

NUTCRACKER
★★★

Shake:

⅓ Nut Liqueur
⅓ Peppermint Schnapps
⅓ Cream Liqueur

A great Christmas holiday shooter.

Shots & Shooters

OREO COOKIE
★★★★

Shake:

½ Dark Cocao
⅓ Vodka
⅙ Cream

An outstanding creation if I ever tasted one.
(Thanks Denise)

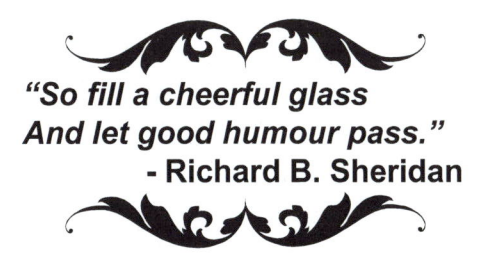

*"So fill a cheerful glass
And let good humour pass."*
- Richard B. Sheridan

ORGASM
★★★★

Pour:

⅔ Peppermint Schnapps
⅓ Cream Liqueur

Interesting presentation and an apt name.

Shots & Shooters

P.C.B.
★★★

Shake:

⅓ Peppermint Schnapps
⅓ Orange Liqueur (Cointreau)
⅓ Cream Liqueur (Bailey's)

Be careful with these chemicals.

*"Drink because you are happy
But never because you are miserable."*
- G.K. Chesterton

PEPPERMINT PUSHOVER
★★

Shake:

½ Peppermint Schnapps
½ Vodka

Best when served very cold so shake a little longer.

Shots & Shooters

POPSICLE
★★★

Shake:

⅓ Orange Liqueur
⅓ Apricot Liqueur
⅙ Lime Juice
⅙ Cream

A must on hot days.

*"With this goblet, rich and deep,
I cradle all my woes to sleep."*
— **Tom Moore**

PRAIRIE FIRE
★

Pour:

1 Tequila
Add several drops of Tabasco

Never ordered by a sober person - Ever!

RED JELLY BEAN
★★★

Pour:

⅓ Grenadine
⅓ Tequila
⅓ Licorice Liqueur

No really - they taste like that.

*"The problem with some people is that
When they aren't drunk,
They are sober!"*

— William Butler Yeats

RUSTY SPIKE
★★

Pour:

½ Scotch
½ Drambuie

Could this be where the phrase "getting hammered" comes from?

Shots & Shooters

RYAN'S RUSH
★★★

Shake:

½ Coffee Liqueur
⅓ White Rum
⅙ Cream

One of the original shooters.

"I can resist everything except temptation."
- Oscar Wilde

SAMBUCA - THE ROMAN CLASSIC
★★★

Pour:

1 Sambuca (Luxardo)

Add:
3 Coffee Beans
(Health, Wealth, and Happiness)

Light on fire until the beans are roasted (30 sec.), extinguish, let cool briefly, then down.

Shots & Shooters

SAMBUCA DEPTH CHARGE

★★★

Pour:

1 Glass of your favourite beer, ale or lager

Add:

1 Shot of Sambuca - glass and all

Toast and down in one motion.
Also called a 'Bucca - Beer' (pronounced 'boo-ka').
Closely related to the 'boilermaker'.

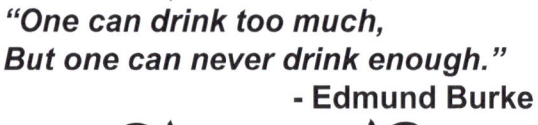

*"One can drink too much,
But one can never drink enough."*
— Edmund Burke

SCHNAPPS

★★★★

Pour or shake:

1 Your favourite flavour schnapps

There are so many great flavours now available it makes the choice difficult.

Shots & Shooters

SCREAMING LIZARD
★

Pour:

½ Chartreuse
½ Tequila

Not a personal favourite but it is popular with "lounge lizards".

"A man hath no better thing under the sun, Than to eat, and to drink, and to be merry."
- Ecclesiastes 8:15

SEVEN FORTY SEVEN
★★★★

Pour:

⅓ Coffee Liqueur
⅓ Nut Liqueur
⅓ Cream Liqueur

Also delicious when shaken.

Shots & Shooters

SEX ON THE BEACH
★★★★★

Shake:

⅓ Peach Schnapps
⅓ Melon Liqueur
⅓ Chambord

There are many different versions of this drink but this is one of my favorites.

*"Drink with impunity -
Or anyone who happens to invite you."*
— Artemus Ward

SICILIAN KISS
★★

Shake:

¾ Cinzano
⅛ Nut Liqueur (Amaretto)
⅛ Lemon Juice

A Mediterranean favourite.

Shots & Shooters

SLIPPERY NIPPLE

★★★★

Pour:

⅔ Licorice Liqueur
⅓ Cream Liqueur

Never shaken.

*"Say anything you like about me,
Except that I drink water."*
— W.C. Fields

SNAKEBITE

★★

Pour:

1 Yukon Jack

Squeeze:

¼ Fresh Lime

A popular Canadian creation.

Shots & Shooters

SPEAKEASY
★★

Shake:

⅔ Gin (Bath-tub variety preferably)
⅓ Cream
Splash Grenadine

For those of you who like to Charleston.

"Let's drink together, friendly and embrace."
- Shakespeare (Henry IV)

SPIKED HEEL
★★★★

Pour:

½ Coffee Liqueur
⅓ Schnapps
⅙ Cream

Also known as a Stiletto.

Shots & Shooters

STRAWBERRY FIELDS
★★★

Shake:

⅓ Banana Liqueur
⅓ Cream Liqueur
⅓ Strawberry Liqueur
Dash of Grenadine

"Living is easy with eyes closed…"

"Nothing relaxes the boys like a good fight."
- Francis 'King' Clancy

TARTAN SPECIAL
★★

Shake:

⅓ Scotch
⅓ Drambuie
⅓ Cream Liqueur

Bonnie Prince Charlie would be proud.

Shots & Shooters

TEST-TUBE BABY
★★★

Pour:

½ Nut Liqueur
½ Tequila

Add:

1-2 drops of cream with a short straw.

"Better a belly burst than a good liquor lost."
- Jonathan Swift

TEQUILA SLAMMER
★★

Pour:

1 Tequila into a 'rocks' glass

Add: 1 Seven Up/Sprite

Cover with hand and rap smartly on table -
drink while effervescing.

Shots & Shooters

TURBO
★

Pour:

⅔ Drambuie
⅓ Peppermint Schnapps

A brutal shooter often used by bartenders to send undesirables home.

---

*"Never exaggerate your faults;
Your friends will attend to that."*
- Robert Edwards

TUTTI FRUITTI PUNCH
★★★

Shake:

⅔ Peach Schnapps
⅓ Cherry Liqueur

And I mean punch!

Shots & Shooters

WATERGATE
★★★★

Shake:

⅓ Coffee Liqueur
⅓ Cream Liqueur
⅙ Peppermint Schnapps
⅙ Orange Liqueur

Actually invented by a bartender whose name is Richard Nixon.

"Sophistication is the art of getting drunk With the right people."

— Walter Winchell

WINDMILL
★★★

Shake:

⅓ Chocolate Liqueur
⅓ Apricot Liqueur
⅓ Advokaat

A knockout.

Shots & Shooters

X-RAY
★★★

Shake:

⅓ Chocolate Liqueur
⅓ Nut Liqueur
⅓ Brandy

Good right down to your bones.

*"The hang-over became a part of the day
As well allowed for as the Spanish siesta."*
— F. Scott Fitzgerald

ZIPPER
★★

Shake:

⅓ Orange Liqueur
⅓ Tequila
⅓ Cream

No teeth but still there's a bite.

HOT SHOTS

THE TOAST OF THE SEASON

Is 'Old Man Winter' constantly blowing icy north winds in your face? Tired of braving temperatures that inevitably begin with a minus?

Then 'Hot Shots' are for you.

Hot shots are specially designed for winter consumption and should quickly warm you up on the coldest of days. They're created by mixing equal parts of liqueurs with a beverage such as hot chocolate or coffee. These two ounce shooters are then topped off with whipped cream and are guaranteed to warm the cockles of your heart.

"Since God created man upon the face of the earth,
There never was a more downright absurdity
Imposed upon and supported by civilized people,
Than that of absolute abstinence from all intoxicating liquors."

— Reverand Robert Murray 1835

AFTER EIGHT (HOT)

★★★★

Pour:

½ Coffee Liqueur
½ Green Creme de Menthe
1 Hot Chocolate

Shots & Shooters

APOLLO
★★★★★

Pour:

½ Licorice Liqueur
½ Cream Liqueur
1 Hot Chocolate

To the last run of the day and great tanning on the slopes.

"Somebody bet me tonight that I wouldn't remember it."
- Bob Dylan (Opening of his True Confessions tour)

CAMPFIRE
★★★

Pour:

Sambuca
(or any other liqueur that you can light)

Set on fire and have some fun roasting mini-marshmallows on toothpicks and singing appropriate campfire songs.
(Eg. "Show me the way to go home")

Shots & Shooters

CANADA CUP
★★★★

Pour:

½ Canadian Rye Whiskey
½ Coffee Liqueur
1 Coffee

He shoots, she shoots,
- they score.

"Change everything except lovers."
— Voltaire

JACK FROST
★★★★

Pour:

½ Jack Daniels
½ Peppermint Schnapps
1 Hot Chocolate

Prevents nipping at your nose.

Shots & Shooters

KILTWARMER
★★

Pour:

½ Scotch
½ Glayva
1 Coffee

Guaranteed to stop draughts up y'ar kilt, lad.

"As he brews, so shall he drink."
- Ben Jonson

MELTDOWN
★★★

Pour:

½ Cognac
½ Chocolate Liqueur
1 Coffee

To toast the end of the season or the beginning of the last.

Shots & Shooters

MOCHA MAGIC
★★★★★

Pour:

½ Nut Liqueur
½ Peppermint Schnapps
1 Hot Chocolate

Delicious.

*"When the going gets weird,
The weird turn pro."*
- Raoul Duke

MINI MARNIER
★★★

Pour:

1 Orange Liqueur (Grand Marnier)
1 Coffee

The original 'Hot Shot'.

Shots & Shooters

SKI LIFT
★★★★

Pour:

½ Chocolate Liqueur
½ Brandy
1 Hot Chocolate

An 'après ski' special to melt the ice.

> *"Big shots are only little shots Who kept shooting."*
> — Christopher Morley

YETI'S REVENGE
★★★★

Pour:

½ Coffee Liqueur
½ Banana Liqueur
1 Coffee

Seen only briefly.

Shots & Shooters

OUNCES OF PREVENTION TO PREVENT A POUND OF HANGOVER

*"When you can't stand the terrible crashing
Of snowflakes as they hit the ground,
You have had enough."*
— Gerald Barzen

As you may imagine, many a morning I have awoken with a powerful, pounding hangover. To help you prevent this, I offer some advice that, if followed, will reduce your hangover and your misery. (This is advice for before and during your night, for the "morning after" see Hangover Helpers).

★ Have dinner. Don't drink on an empty stomach or you'll pay for it the next day.

★ Snack at some point in the evening.

★ Try to drink fruit drinks rather than carbonated mixers. They provide more minerals, less sugar and usually come with those spiffy little umbrellas.

★ Drink a seltzer or a soda before you retire. If you're out, have water and lots of it.

Shots & Shooters

HANGOVER HELPERS

*"Lord, how my head aches!
What a head have I! It beats as
It would fall in twenty pieces."*
   - Shakespeare (Romeo and Juliet)

Hangovers have been with us since the first Cro Magnon cocktail party. Many bizarre cures have been suggested, tried and evaluated. The process continues today and I thought it was time to shed some light on the more popular solutions to the "morning after".

Realize first of all that you have just flooded yourself with alcohol (you took alcohol in faster than your body could get rid of it). In addition you've probably taken in an additional dose of sugar if you were drinking shooters or mixers.

So plan on making the "day after" a slow one. Rest up, down some A.S.A. and get plenty of non-alcoholic liquid into the old system. Don't plan on changing the world too much and assume the classic couch potato position.

For extremely serious cases you may want to try one of the following suggested cures, but remember:

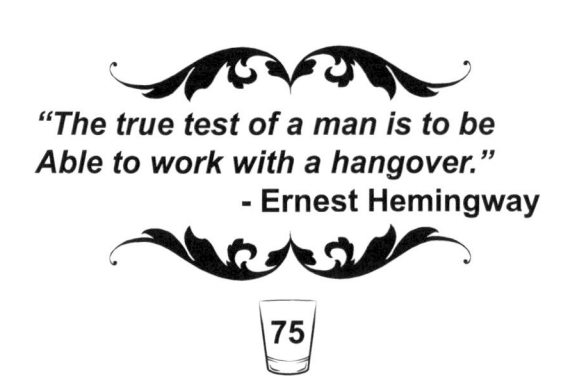

*"The true test of a man is to be
Able to work with a hangover."*
   - Ernest Hemingway

Shots & Shooters

HANGOVER HELPERS

WATER & VITAMINS

This method involves doubling or tripling your normal vitamin intake and drinking as much cold water as you can stand. This will flush all those nasty little toxins out that you've spent collecting the previous night. The vitamins will replenish those lost as you attempt to clean out your system. A word of caution - don't go too hard on the vitamins as your kidneys have probably been through enough.

SUCCESS RATE

Fairly successful if you have the day off or you don't have much moving to do. Otherwise you could get too waterlogged and won't last too long.

"Never trust a brilliant idea
Until it survives the hangover."
- Jimmy Breslin

Shots & Shooters

HANGOVER HELPERS

OXYGEN

This is one of the best kept secrets in the food and beverage industry. Restaurants frequently carry oxygen tanks in case of a patron having a heart attack. I have never in my fourteen years in the industry seen it used for this purpose. I have, however, seen it used on many occasions to help a person get over a severe hangover. It is my understanding that it is also used for this purpose by medical students and paramedics. With this in mind, you probably need a friend in the right field but five minutes "on the mask" can change your entire day. Small 'blasts' or booster shots' may be needed throughout the day in severe cases.

SUCCESS RATE
Great relief but access to an oxygen tank can prove difficult.

"There is nothing wrong with sobriety In moderation."
— John Ciardi

Shots & Shooters

HANGOVER HELPERS

PRAIRIE OYSTER

An old recipe with many variations all designed to replenish vitamins through a raw egg yolk. Choose the type of liquor or liqueur to suit your tastes (using the "Hair of the Dog" helper) or make up some beef bouillon.

MIX
One ounce of liquor, liqueur or bouillon. Dash of red wine vinegar, worcestershire sauce and cayenne powder.

POUR
The entire mixture of an egg and swallow without breaking the yolk.

SUCCESS RATE
Some people swear by this helper but it seems to depend on what and how much you drank the night before. Options, other than bouillon, include clamato and tomato juice.

*"It's better to have had a few mornings after
Than never to have had a night before."*
— Jack Wasserman

Shots & Shooters

HANGOVER HELPERS

HAIR OF THE DOG

This "cure" seems utterly illogical yet it provides psychological relief to some. It involves drinking additional amounts of whatever it was you drank the night before. The name comes from an old superstition that dates back to Roman times. It was believed that if bitten by a dog, the possible infection would be controlled if a hair from that same dog was consumed. They had no penicillin in those days so even a minor bite often proved fatal. Today many people insist that it's only the first drink (hair?) that's difficult to get down. After that you feel great - or so they say.

SUCCESS RATE

After many discussions with believers in this cure, there appears to be some kind of mental satisfaction involved. This could be from the power of positive thinking or - and this is more likely - from the early effects of the alcohol consumed. My recommendation is that if you must employ this helper, stick with lighter drinks such as caesars, spritzers, coolers and champagne cocktails. Your body will appreciate it in the long run.

"Always remember that I have taken more out of alcohol Than alcohol has taken out of me."

— Winston Churchill

Shots & Shooters

STOCKING YOUR SHOOTER BAR

*"A bumper of good liquor,
Will end a contest quicker,
Than Justice, Judge or Vicar."*
- Richard Sheridan

Once you decide to start your own shooter bar, don't go out and buy a stock of expensive liqueurs. Start slowly and experiment - the best are not always the most expensive.

This way you will gain a greater understanding of both liqueurs and shooters, their properties and distinctive tastes.

It is recommended that the following list be used in preparing any "serious" shooter bar.

1 BOTTLE OF EACH: *(750ml)*

Coffee Liqueur	Tequila
Chocolate Liqueur	Parfait A'mour
Orange Liqueur	Nut Liqueur
Cream Liqueur	Licorice Liqueur
Banana Liqueur	Peppermint Schnapps
Fruit Liqueur	Favourite Flavoured Schnapps

NOTE: One Bottle = 25 Shots = 25 Shooters

STOCKING YOUR SHOOTER BAR

If you're on a budget, you should be able to get started for less than $100, as many of the liqueurs are available in the half size of 375ml.

If that's too rich for your blood, have a shooter party where the guests bring a bottle of each type. It's considered good taste to offer bed and breakfast to your overindulgent guests. Be prepared for this or have a designated (sober) driver.

Large common cups holding sever shooters are popular at parties and bars alike. Known as "Loving Cups", these drinks are consumed by several people using straws, in a race to the bottom of the glass. The concept dates back several centuries when large common bowls of spirits were passed around the table at festivals, weddings and other celebrations.

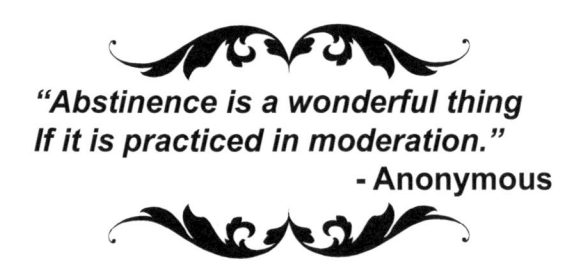

*"Abstinence is a wonderful thing
If it is practiced in moderation."*
— Anonymous

Shots & Shooters

*"Now is not the end.
It is not even the beginning of the end.
It is, perhaps, the end of the beginning."*
— Winston Churchill

THANK YOU...

...for buying my "*little*" cocktail recipe book. If you enjoyed this book, could I be so bold as to request a review for my book on Amazon?

https://bit.ly/shots-and-shooters

Much appreciated and make it a great day!

- Bazooka Joe

Printed in Great Britain
by Amazon